Journey

Journey

Journey

A collection of heartfelt poems written by

Gail Tennyson Hicks

To order additional copies of this book, contact:
Xlibris Corporation
1-888-795-4274
www.Xlibris.com
Orders@Xlibris.com
26157

CONTENTS

I dedicate this book to my loving parents, George and Margaret,
whose support and encouragement never lacked;
to my darling husband, Bo,
who showed me that dreams do come true;
and to my wonderful sons Little Bo and Royce,
who love me in spite of myself.

ACKNOWLEDGEMENTS

When I was a little girl, on Christmas mornings I would stumble into our living room, bleary-eyed from lack of sleep the night before (who sleeps on Christmas Eve?). As I would round the corner into the room, my fatigue would vanish and my eyes would widen at the sight of all my toys under the tree. They sat waiting, assembly complete and any required batteries inserted, ready to play with me. That's what it was like growing up—there was always something special around the bend. My mother and father created and sustained that magical environment in our family, and the feeling stayed with me through adulthood. I thank them for always being there for me, for reading every story and poem I wrote, and for keeping the praise and encouragement flowing.

To my husband Bo: thank you for holding my hand and calming my fears, for listening and understanding, for making me laugh, and for loving me completely and unconditionally. After years of admiring the successful marriages of other people, our marriage is now admired by many, and that is because of you (and sometimes me, too).

To my sons Little Bo and Royce: thank you for giving me the opportunity to be a mother to you. After seven years, I am still learning and have a long way to go, but with your love and support I will get it right one day! God is still working on me; thank you for your patience.

To Auntie Vivian: thank you for being my surrogate mother-in-law. You welcomed me from the start, and your warmth and wisdom carry me through each day.

Thank you to my sisters Jacqui, Ann, Mary, JoAnn, Marsha, Judy; and my new sisters Cheri, Deb, Margo, and Nunie: you set an example of strength, independence, and womanhood that I try hard to follow.

To my brothers George Jr., Joseph, Mike; and my new brother Chuck: you are an example of what I should have been looking for in a man all along. And you too, Don; even though you are my nephew, you feel like a brother to me. Thanks for cheering me on ALL of the time.

To my nieces pieces: Ree Ree, Kat, Moni, and Dee Dee: all these years I thought I was helping to raise you, but you ended up helping to raise me. I wanna be like YOU when I grow up!

Next, a shout-out to my sisterfriends Poomie, Lynn, Jack, Rosalind, Leonore, Ndeye, Yvonne, Joyce, Chris, Gwendy, Karen, Ofie, Faye, and Beanie: thank you for showing me what true friendship is all about.

Then there's my AAIB friendship crew: Lisa, Suzy, D-Etta, Max, Edna, and Tijanna. You inspire me, and I love and admire you tremendously. Special thanks to Tee for helping me edit, and for being my sounding board without (too much) complaint!

And to the rest of my family and friends: just because I did not name you does not mean that you are any less special to me. You are the clock that keeps me ticking, and I love you all.

INTRODUCTION

Welcome to my first book! I thank God for giving me the gift of written expression, my family and friends for giving me the courage to finally finish this book, and you for taking the time to read it. What is a life's journey? I believe it's what we need to go through in order to grow, learn, or change. It's how we get from Point A to Point B in our lives. This book is appropriately titled *Journey* because it takes you, the reader, down some of the roads I have traveled thus far in my life. Each chapter represents a different journey, and each journey represents specific times of my life, recounting some of the precious joys and pains of that time. It includes the wonderful, the exciting, the funny, the painful, the exhilarating, the dramatic, the excruciating. It's all here!

Journey to Love—the poems in this chapter speak frankly about the destructive relationships in my past, and bring to light some important issues such as physical and emotional abuse, third-party relationship drama, and the low self-esteem and self-doubt that I have struggled with. It also speaks to how I finally came to realize that I had to matter to myself before I could matter to someone else. Once I started loving myself, my dreams about marriage, sensuality, sexual fulfillment, and finding the perfect love for me came to fruition.

Journey to Family—this chapter pays homage to the family, the good and bad, the weird and the wonderful. It also honors my parents, who did a superb job of raising my eight siblings and me. When I became a mother to my husband's children, I learned to appreciate how challenging my parents job was and can only hope to rub elbows with the example that they set. Also in this chapter are tributes to special relatives who have passed on: my grandmother, my sister, my niece, and my father. The loss of each was devastating to me, but the most devastating of all was the death of my father in 2001. His death set off a chain of events that threw my family into a terrible storm that some are still weathering through today.

Journey to Pride—this chapter celebrates my African American heritage and the pride that it instills in me. We have come a long way, but our journey is one that is sometimes filled with doubt, anger, mistrust (sometimes of each other!) and that nagging feeling that no matter what, we are not good enough. Some of us are still trying to rise above stereotypes and narrow-minded people. It hurts my heart that even today the kids at my son's school call him the N-word. But we are overcoming every day. And we will not stop.

Journey to Faith—this chapter celebrates my belief in God and His son Jesus. It really is true that through Him all things are possible. I don't know anyone who has gotten anywhere without the Lord. I have seen His miracles, and I have seen how the lives of those I care about have been changed through Him. He has touched my life in ways that only He can, and I am grateful. God's blessings are everywhere, and I am blessed and proud to be a child of God.

Journey to Me—this final chapter is my favorite because it celebrates who I am, just as I am, without apologizing. It also addresses the perceptions that others have tried to project onto me, and my response to those perceptions. No one will ever make me doubt myself again. I love me, and that's the take-home message of this chapter— for all of us to love and appreciate ourselves just as we are, draw those who accept us to us, and rid ourselves of all negative influences and people.

Our journeys are our tickets through life. We may stumble and fall along the way, but our journeys help us to learn from our mistakes so that the next journey is a little easier. My hope is that after reading about my journeys, you will be inspired to make the most of yours. For without the journey, the destination is unreachable.

Chapter 1

Journey to
Love

"Love is like time—too precious to waste."—*Gail Tennyson Hicks*

Dirty Little Secret

As his hand once again
flew to my face
I almost felt deserving
almost
until it dawned on me
that someone
so kind and loving
would never deserve such cruelty
it dawned on me
that I was the victim
of his lies
of his deceit
of him
but too late again
the imprint left
angry red marks

across my cheek
but they were nothing
compared to
the angry marks scattered
across my heart
but I still stayed
I stayed because
I was ashamed
I stayed because
I didn't want anyone to know
I stayed because
I didn't know how to leave
I stayed at the expense
of my happiness
of my peace of mind
of me
I stayed.

The Dark Side of Love

Sometimes love can be bitter
sometimes love can hurt so
and when the pain becomes physical
that's when it is time to let go

For love shouldn't hurt so badly
that your bones begin to break
you should never have to wonder
whether or not your life is at stake

The first time shame on him
but the next time shame on you
how many times will it happen
before you will know what to do?

Will "I'm sorry" ever get tired?
and "forgive me" become a joke?
when will you reject the words
"I love you" that afterwards he spoke?

It's time to take the steps
to free yourself from misery
loving him won't make a difference
you'll just suffer constantly

When it's a matter of your life
close your heart and lock the door
for you can love him all you want
but you must love yourself much more.

Check Mate

We were happy
at first
the fun we had
was big
the times we shared
were special
and our love shined
like white diamonds
but something happened
we stopped having fun
the times were
no longer special
and the love
turned out to be
only gold-plated
all signs that
I had made
the cardinal mistake
of being with
someone else's mate.
Oops.

Let Her Go

How can I love you
when you won't let her go?
you should have told her goodbye
before you told me hello

You told her all about me
when I told you you shouldn't
you told her all about us
when you promised you wouldn't

I know you have kids together
and that you go back some years
that doesn't give her the right
to meddle and interfere

How can I love you
when you won't let her go?
why do you always tell her yes
when you should tell her no?

You wouldn't want me to do it
but for you the rules bend
you cannot be an exception
just because you're good friends

This is not about jealously
but what's right and what's fair
she has lied and manipulated
still you show her you care

How can I love you
when you won't let her go?
where is the respect
you'd expect me to show?

You always defend her
no matter what she does
as well as wanting what is
you're still wanting what was

I have told you and told you
that you can't play both sides
either you play ball in her court
or you play ball in mine

How can I love you
when you won't let her go?
to her you're accommodating
to me you're disloyal

Where is the honesty
that you know I deserve?
you would feel the same way
if the tables were turned

She's playing game after game
with your blessing it seems
instead of setting her straight
you give in to her schemes

How can I love you
when you won't let her go?
how can we build a life
and expect love to grow?

You need to clean house
and that bridge has to burn
I'm offering complete love
I want the same in return

You must make up your mind
one plus one is not three
is it your past with her
or your future with me?

How can I love you
when you won't let her go?
the answer is simple . . .
it is Impossible.

Love Gives

Why don't you call me anymore
or do the things you did before
Is it something that I said
or are you playing with my head

It's funny how you've changed
after my life I've rearranged
you played a most important part
and now you're playing with my heart

Why do you want more but give less
and leave me to wonder and guess
as if my loss would be your gain
you take great pleasure from my pain

Your word now means nothing more
than old news the day before
where love looked as if it bloomed
has turned to salt rubbed in a wound

It's time for me to step aside
for the "real you" has arrived
I hope you learn from this mistake
that love gives more than it should take.

Move On

He left you
the Bible said it was
supposed to last forever
but the Bible
in all its blessed glory
often represents
the best-case scenario
imposing perfection
on an imperfect world
the reality
is that love has rights
just like we do
love has a right
    to change its mind
love has a right
    to change its course
love has a right
    to grow, stay, or go away
—and anyway
why would you want
to be locked into forever

if love is gone
and happiness severed
so don't cry—don't hate
thank him
because he did you
a favor
and you are free now
to savor
the sweet taste of freedom
    the looking forward
    the leaving behind
    the out of sight
    the out of mind
and eventually heart
time now to make
yourself a new start
you deserve much more
than what he had in store
so let him go forever
then lock your heart's door
and move on.

Heartache

I've learned from past experience about heartache and pain
the agony of finding love, then losing it again
loneliness is catching and can eat your heart away
you wonder how you'll ever make it through another day

Time appears to stand still as you wade through all the sorrow
the hope of feeling better dwindles as you face tomorrow
it seems like everyone you know is happy and content
depression finds a home in you and makes its long descent

You try to find a reason to rebuild your shattered life
it just seems so much easier to let it pass you by
the sleepless nights, the empty days, the silent telephone
the constant ache reminding you that you are now alone

Friends and family want to help, but they don't understand
the pain you feel is much too deep for them to comprehend
it can't be cured with kindness, it can't be fed with pitied love
the only thing that will help is a prayer to God above

Pray for strength and guidance, pray for inner transformation
pray for the will to learn how to accept your situation
reach inside your heart and find the source of all your tears
bring about the truth that has you trapped inside your fears

Understand yourself and you'll be on your way to healing
if you sacrifice the lie, the truth will be well worth revealing
one day you will be ready to give love another try
until then, concentrate on telling your heartache goodbye.

Guess What?

you abused me

still i loved you

you lied to me

still i believed you

you neglected me

still i needed you

you rejected me

still i wanted you

you left me

still i missed you

i know what that says

about you

but what does that

say about me?

i think it says

i value you more

than i value myself

but guess what?

Not Anymore.

Self Respect

I gave, you took, and when I looked
inside my heart was breaking
yet even so, could not let go
my need for you painstaking

I coaxed, you quit, and then you hit
more than my spirit broken
my shattered pride burned deep inside
"I'm sorry" rarely spoken

I asked, you hid, the things you did
made fools of both of us
promises sold, new lies were told
regained then lost my trust

I stayed, you ran, can't understand
problems you would not face
betrayal grew, and then I knew
my faith in you erased

I was, you seemed, destroyed our dream
the secrets you still hold
you turned your back, honesty lacked
the truth remains untold

I loved, you charmed, my soul unarmed
but I was never first
I compromised, you criticized
the bad things just got worse

I learned, you lost, look what it cost
we couldn't make love last
your word you gave, but lies remained
your past would not stay past

I guess I know, time to let go
this phase of my life done
with no regret, my mind is set
my self-respect has won.

Left Turn

Driving down
Chase Avenue
not thinking
about where
I'm supposed
to be going
I turn right
instead of left
and end up in
an alley
when
my tire fails
probably
a rusty nail
suddenly—
from out of
nowhere
he blew
like a tornado
charging through
my stormy life
he fixed my tire
then he fixed
my soul
I'm so glad
I never made
that left turn.

Promise

Take me
> for I am yours and
> I give myself to you

Touch me
> for no one else
> can go where you can

Kiss me
> for my lips
> were made for yours

Hold me
> in your strong arms
> I feel so safe

Respect me
> treat me as you
> want to be treated

Trust me
> for I will never
> betray your faith

Cherish me
> make me the exception
> to all your rules

Understand me
> for I am not perfect
> nor do I expect you to be

Support me
> stand by my side
> even when I'm wrong

Love me
> like you've never loved before
> fully
> completely
> ultimately.

My Ebony Dream

Now I lay me down
to sleep
Ebony dreams are mine
to keep
I had one
the night before
when true love came
to my front door
he kissed me
as I let him in
his strong arms
held me deep within
we laughed, we talked,
we snuggled close
our dreams and wishes
we bespoke
we took a nice hot bath
for two

then we did
what lovers do
made sweet love
the whole night long
and then he sang to me
a song
of how his heart
was now made whole
by loving me
he'd found his soul
we fell asleep
in afterglow
until the sun
began to show
when I awoke
my Ebony dream
was lying right there
next to me.

More

Come on in

let me help you

with your coat

dinner is simmering

a hot bubble bath

is running

and sweet sounds

are playing.

Let me rub away

your long day

and ease you into

a long night

of pleasure

Let me relieve

all of your tension

and put you in

erotic suspension

and ecstasy

I will make you

never want to leave

I will give you everything

you need

and then . . .

I'll give you

more.

The Dance

His touch was
soft and gentle
caressing my heart
as well as
my breast
I touched him back
gliding my warm
silky hands over
his body
reaching him
in places and ways
he never imagined
making him moan
with painful pleasure
he kissed me
over and over
tasting like hot love
on a cool day
quenching my thirst
yet driving my need
for him
his eyes were beautiful
as he gazed at me
with hunger
passion
desire
and ultimate love
I could tell
he was ready
to be one with me
as I was ready
to be one
with him

So we danced
the love dance
keeping time
with each other
and to the growing
rhythm within
going higher
higher
higher than either
of us had ever been
until we both
found release
somewhere far past
fireworks
ringing bells
and Cloud Nine
In the afterglow
I cried
tears of joy
and he held me
so close I could
feel his heartbeat
he kissed me
with tenderness
understanding
happiness
then he kissed me
with hunger
passion
desire
and the love dance
began
again . . .

Marriage is Not

Marriage is not a book
that you can read
when you feel like it
then close and put away
when you don't
But it is a favorite story
packed with your precious
moments and memories
that you read over and over again
never tiring of its predictability
and somehow finding something
new and exciting each time

Marriage is not a long distance call
where you can talk as long
as you want, then
hang up when you've said all you have to say
But it is the most intimate conversation
between God, yourself and
the one you love
and every time you communicate
you strengthen your love
and deepen your understanding
for one another

Marriage is not a board game
where someone is always
taking and owing
and where there is usually
a winner and a loser
But it is a challenge
and a constant struggle
to make sure you always win
with each other
and give in
to each other

Marriage is not a bank
where you can make
deposits, withdrawals, exact loans,
then close the account
when it suits you
But it is an institution
where you invest your
love, time, hopes, dreams
a life-long savings account of joy
a vault where you keep
your most precious valuable person
protected from harm or misuse

Marriage is not a new coat
that you wear when its cold
then take off when its not
But it is something that
is always in fashion
with who you are
and you wear it proudly
because it's always in style
it governs your actions,
your reactions, your thoughts,
your plans, and your decisions.

Marriage is not a movie
that you can watch
when you feel like it
then put in a new movie
when you get tired of the old one
But it is a beautiful drama
with you and your love
as the main characters
and you both work together
to make sure that
your love story never ends.

A New Beginning

What a special day it was
the day when I met you
God answered all my prayers
and made you my dream come true

So lovingly you've shown me
happiness so very sweet
before you I was whole
but now I am complete

You bring peace to my soul
a gladness to my heart
such a perfect basis
for a brand new life to start

And in return I'm offering
more love than you've ever known
a chance to share your true self
and never be alone

Our life will be a good one
with respect as the foundation
the rewards will be so sweet
filled with loving compensation

Together we'll face challenge
and together we'll face change
together we will struggle
as our futures rearrange

But these are all life's changes
and I know they're for the best
we'll take care of each other
God will take care of the rest

What a special day it was
the day my heart was spinning
because you came into my life
and offered me a new beginning.

Home

When I turn the key
and step inside
leaving the world
and its problems behind
I see you waiting
with open arms
nothing else matters
but your sweet charm
your kiss warms me
through and through
your eyes tell me
what you want to do
give me, take me
all nightlong
heartbeats playing
love's sweet song
undress me, caress me
please take it slow
the way that I like it
is the way that you know
you thrill me, you fill me
with love so complete
your touch drives me crazy
and leaves me so weak
desire is urgent
and passion won't wait
this can't be by chance
it must be by fate
we're perfect together
a real dream come true
nothing else matters
except coming home
to you.

Core

At the core of my inner being
there is a gentle peace that calms me
a serendipity that charms me
a passion that ignites me

At the core of my deepest thoughts

there is a Queendom of Consciousness

that makes me believe in dreams

and long for their reality

At the core of my existence
there is a very basic need
to be loved, needed, wanted
it is the essence of my life

At the core of my inner being

at the core of my deepest thoughts

at the core of my existence

there is you.

My Dream Come True
(Wedding Vows)

I have no expectations
of where our road will lead
I only know I love you
and that we were meant to be
The storms of life
will come and go
regardless of the season
but we will weather all of them
and love will be the reason

You will never have to wonder
if my love for you will last
you will never have to worry
about the future or the past
Our lives will be a blending
of two hearts, spirits, and minds
where two best friends in love
will share a rare and precious find

Marriage is like a garden
and it must be grown with care
the weeds should be so few
and the flowers—more to spare
Your smile is my priority
your needs are mine to meet
support and understanding
you will always find in me

I commit to love you more
with the passing of each day
I commit my heart and soul
to loving you in every way
As we serve God and each other
this is my promise to you
our forever starts today
because you are
my dream come true.

MMHB

He is pure happiness
    tasting like
    sunshine, fresh air,
    and sweet, tart, juicy
    pomegranates
He is pure satisfaction
    on a stick
    and I'm the only one
    who can have a lick
    or two
He oozes masculinity
    even while scrambling eggs
    or creating one of his many
    culinary masterpieces
His is the warmth in my belly
    the peanut butter to my jelly
    the king to my queen
    and everything in between
His confidence astounds me
    his faith in God is unwavering
    he possesses strength
    beyond the physical
    and energy way past the mystical

He loves me unconditionally
    and cloaks me with his dreams
    our bestfriendhood it thrives
    and his sense of humor—so funny
He's intelligent beyond all teachings
    generous, kind, and thoughtful
    he can fix just about anything
    his big, strong hands—a marvel
Who is he, you might wonder
    you can guess and try to ponder
    but oh yes, he does exist
    I'll introduce if you insist
He is paradise, heaven, and cloud nine
    and I assure you, he's all mine
    I'll tell you now so you will know
    His name is **Mister My Husband, Bo**.

Chapter 2

Journey to **Family**

"The flame of family never extinguishes."—Gail Tennyson Hicks

Dear Mom . . .

By the time you read this
I will love you even more
more than yesterday
and all the days before

For each day that I live
I thank God for blessing me
with a mom so dear as you
who's as sweet as sweet can be

Your thought-provoking words
have made me more aware
your loving, caring ways
have always been right there

Thank you for the lessons
that were worth the learning of
thank you for the happiness
and unconditional love

You said it to me once
and now I will say it too
with all the love I have inside
my heart beats for you.

Dear Dad . . .

The world is full of fathers
but none as great as you
you put so much love and energy
into everything you do

You've always been my hero
the true epitome of a man
although everyone admires you
I'm still your biggest fan

Your sound advice has taught me
that true strength comes from within
I trust those words completely
because they're from my greatest friend

Thank you for your guidance
it led me through this life
it taught me how to be successful
in a world so full of strife

If I am half the person you are
it makes my heart so glad
for I know that I am truly blessed
to have you as my dad.

Parenthood

The bond that exists
    between parent and child
    is solid and strong
    yet loving and mild
    it starts at conception
    and continues through life
    in the toughest of times
    it is there as a guide
From the terrible twos
    to the terrible teens
    a parent's love challenges
    all of these things
    to help with the joys,
    pains, troubles, and fears
    that will follow each child
    throughout his or her years
The lessons of life
    will be better learned
    when children are reared
    with love and concern

the morals instilled
while they live at home
will determine how well
they succeed on their own
Sometimes you'll be proud
sometimes you'll be pained
sometimes the love that you share
will be strained
there may be broken bones
and report cards done well
there may be teenage romance
and plenty of dates from hell
But through it all
one thing will be clear
parenthood is something
beholden and dear
and as each child
becomes an adult
be proud of your work
and watch the results.

Dear Daughter . . .

I wish I could tell you all that you'll need
to go far in this world and to always succeed
but the best I can do is make sure you know
that I love you

I wish I could teach you all about life
from becoming a woman to being a good wife
but the best I can do is share with you
my life's experiences

I wish I could shield you from all of life's hurts
but that won't make things better for you, only worse
the best I can do is be there for you
when you need me

I wish I could show you which path you should take
but that's a decision that you'll have to make
the best I can do is support your endeavors
whether right or wrong

I wish I could give you the knowledge you'll seek
when you're up against problems that render you weak
but the best I can do is advise and instruct
and hope that you'll do the right thing

I've given you life and now you must live it
use my love as a guide and you'll surely benefit
the best I can do is make sure you know
that I'm always on your side.

Dear Son . . .

I wish I could tell you that life won't be hard
and the things you'll encounter will not leave you scarred
but the best I can do is set an example
of inner strength and pride

I wish I could teach you how not to give in
to temptations that turn good boys into bad men
but the best I can do is make sure you know
right from wrong

I wish I could shield you from prejudice and hate
because they will try hard to determine your fate
the best I can do is provide you with courage
to overcome them

I wish I could show how you could go farther
by being a good man, husband and father
the best I can do is set an example
that you'll want to follow

I wish I could give you your mind's desire
to expand your options and always reach higher
but the best I can do is give encouragement
when you need it

I've given you life and the sky is your limit
you can do anything if you put your mind to it
the best I can do is be so very proud
that you are my son.

You'll Come Around
(Ode to Teenagers)

You may not like us sometimes
    for being so hard on you
    but when life becomes
    an immovable mountain
    and we've taught you
    how to climb,
    you'll come around.

You may resent us sometimes
    for pushing you so much
    but when life tries
    to push you down
    and we've taught you
    how to push back,
    you'll come around.

You may hate it here sometimes
    under our roof and our rules
    but when you find yourself
    at the mercy of your landlord
    and we've taught you
    how to comply,
    you'll come around.

You may think we expect too much
    and want you to be perfect
    but when life expects
    so much more from you
    and we've taught you
    how to deliver,
    you'll come around.

You may think you don't need us
    and the lessons we give freely
    but when life offers you
    nothing without a price
    and we've taught you
    how to pay it,
    you'll come around.

We'll be waiting.

Yellow Rose

Cradled in

his grandmother's arms

the baby slept

calmed by her voice

soothed by her touch

secured by her love

As she held

her first grandson

her mind slipped

into the past

remembering when

she once held

her own son,

who looked

just like this one

Cherishing the bond

between mother and son

together they had come so far

and now

they would go

even farther

because of his child

her new yellow rose.

For The Boys

This is just a thank you
to two special boys I know
one of them is Royce
and the other, Little Bo

When you came into my life
my heart just opened wide
for in you both I found a love
that cannot be denied

Your laughter makes me smile
your smiles—they melt my heart
your hugs are just the best
and your drawings—works of art

I offer you a place
that you can call your home
I offer you the promise
that you'll never be alone

I'll always be here for you
on that you can depend
for I will always love you
and I will always be your friend

I thank you both so very much
for making my life complete
I hope you know in me you'll find
strength, love, and family.

I Refuse

I refuse to say goodbye
instead I'm going to
remember
all the wonderful times
all the fun we had
and your smile

I refuse to say goodbye
instead I'll make a
scrapbook
full of memories
of you and your time
here with us

I refuse to say goodbye
instead I will celebrate
the life you lived
and be eternally grateful
that I was
a part of it

I refuse to say goodbye
but when I do
it won't be forever.

Julia

I remember special times
that we used to share
how we wrote each other letters
and how I loved to brush her hair

She'd talk to me for hours
about life and how she lived it
her tales so fascinating
her stories all so vivid

Her hands could hold the past
and its lessons she taught me
her eyes could see the future
and the hope that it would bring

Her spirit was full of laughter
her heart was full of love
her soul was full of family
all gifts from God above

We all wept tears of sorrow
the day God called her home
remembering with gladness
the love that she had shown

Now she watches over us
protecting us from strife
we still cherish every memory
we still celebrate her life

I loved her with my heart and soul
and miss her with the same
the best grandmother in the world
Julia was her name.

Jacqui

She was funny and crazy
with a laugh so contagious
adventuresome, outgoing
daring, outrageous

She was so full of vigor
and lived life at its best
never stopping to brood
never stopping to rest

She was constantly moving
all the time on the go
caring for everyone
even those she did not know

She was devoted to her children
always there for them
and cherished by her family
like a rare and precious gem

She was a talented writer
her poetry so moving
it reflected her faith
and was so very soothing

She was thoughtful and giving
always trying to please
thinking of others
and meeting their needs

She was a beautiful woman
both inside and out
with a strong sense of self
and no sense of doubt

She loved God so fiercely
and He was her light
at the end of the tunnel
at the end of her fight

In my heart she remains
never leaving my thoughts
I remember with love
the pure joy that she brought

She was all of these things
and each day I miss her
she was all of these things
and she was my sister.

Our Angel Karyn

One day God sent down an angel

to live with us on earth for a while

He called this angel Karyn

and gave her a beautiful smile

While here she was loved by all

and cherished by others still

but as time went on sickness took hold

and Karyn became very ill

God saw that she was suffering

so He called her home to rest

she is free from any pain now

and happy in His loving nest

We will miss our angel Karyn

but her suffering has ceased

it is so comforting to know

that she is finally at peace.

My Father

What can I say about a father
    so wonderful and dear
    who always had a shoulder
    who always had an ear

What can I say about a father
    whose laughter was contagious
    he loved to tease and joke
    his sense of humor so outrageous

What can I say about a father
    who was always there for me
    who always took the time
    to help me see things truthfully

What can I say about a father
    with a heart made out of gold
    filled with stories of his life
    that he so often told

What can I say about a father
    who everyone admired
    he was fearless and invincible
    all who knew him were inspired

What can I say about a father
    who loved his family dearly
    we were everything to him
    anyone could see that clearly

What can I say about a father
    who was just the very best?
    I can say he was MY father
    and for that, I'm truly blessed.

The Lost Minds

Daddy died
and people lost their minds
never had I seen that side
of my family
my greatest source of pride
never had I known such
greed, selfishness, anger, mistrust
to fill me with a growing disgust
it was as if I were seeing them
for the very first time
the faces I grew up with
suddenly as unfamiliar
as a foreign language
something I could neither combat
nor comprehend
They used their pain
as chisels
to expose the pain
of others
their pettiness and jealousy grew
sprouting up
from depths unknown

a rotting stew
in the kitchen of my soul
they felt entitled
to receive
when they never even gave
a damn
and who stole the honey baked ham?
I didn't know that he was the link
that held the illusion in place
like a sail holds a boat
steady
I wanted their masks to go back on
I wanted the illusion to be the reality
and the poisonous erosion
only a bad dream
but even bad dreams come true
and I could be asleep for years
yet forever be awake to the fact that
Daddy died
people lost their minds
I still cry.

November 22nd

Happy Birthday, Dad
remember how I used
to say that to you
and you would say
"It is?" because you
didn't remember
that it was your birthday?

Happy Birthday, Dad
remember how we used
to all come over to the house
and shower you
with love and gifts
while you sat in Your Chair
loving all the attention?

Happy Birthday, Dad
remember how you used
to open every gift
and no matter what it was, say,
"Oh, that's pre-tayyyy!"
as if it was the greatest thing
and then we'd never
see those gifts again?

Happy Birthday, Dad
remember how Mom used
used to bake you a cake
and cook a special dinner
that you always ate too much of
then you'd sit back in Your Chair
and fall asleep?

Happy Birthday, Daddy
I will always remember
this day for you.

Love, Snugglepuss.

Chapter 3

Journey to
Pride

"Pride is the first thing people should notice about you."
—Gail Tennyson Hicks

Black Boy

Black boy,
why you working
at not working?
living at not living?
trying not to try?

Don't you know
ain't nobody
gonna give you
nuthin?

Black boy,
why you dreaming
about being?
Being without seeing?
Choosing not to have
a choice?

Don't you know
you gotta make
your own
breaks?

Black boy,
you need to look
around
past your self-imposed
limitations
past the judgment
of your
so-called friends
past the irresistible urge
to fail.

WAKE UP
to the opportunities
that surround you
REACH OUT
to hope and freedom
GRAB HOLD
of success and
recognition.
It's a new day,
Black boy.

Beautiful Black Man

Beautiful Black Man,
wherever you are
my super hero
my shining star

So fragile your ego
so strong your libido
with pride so incredible
success is inevitable

Beautiful Black Man,
always you will be
one of the best things
to happen to me

Your depth of intelligence
defies social negligence
your eyes tell a story
of struggle and glory

Beautiful Black Man,
whatever you do
know that my spirit
is always with you

Our past can't escape
the identity rape
but it's time now to heal
what past struggles reveal

Beautiful Black Man,
it's not just for you
the pain that you feel
is felt by me, too

Let's honor each other
above any other
the future is better
if we stick together.

The Power of CAN

When they say I won't
that's when I know I will
when they say get moving
that's when I stand still

When they say I shouldn't
that's when I know I shall
when they say keep quiet
that's when I know to tell

When they act reserved
that's when I become bold
when they say I'm too hot
that's when I become cold

When they say go one way
that's when I go another
when they say do this
that's when I do the other

When they say sit down
that's when I stand up
when they want to argue
that's when I rebut

When they act confused
that's when I understand
when they say I can't
that's when I know I CAN.

March On

Where are you going?
hell, I don't know
my dignity severed
my pride low
gotta march on.
It's cloudy outside
nature's gonna cry
can't sit here and worry
how I'm gonna git by
gotta march on.
Gotta git up and do
what they said I couldn't
gotta right to succeed
when they thought I wouldn't
gotta march on.
Which path? What road?
it really don't matter
gotta stay on my feet
beat up and battered
gotta march on.
When I git there I'll sing
and praise the day
that the sunshine came
and the clouds went away
gotta march on.

Racism

Now is the time
to undo the crimes
that were done
to our brothers and sisters
crimes of hatred, mistrust,
collusion, disgust
that clung to their hides
like cold blisters

Let's not point the finger
or let the past linger
polluting our
present and future
but hope that somehow
the time that is now
will bring change
as a permanent suture

If we look inside
holding on to our pride
we might find that
the pain could be duller
let's pray for the day
that racism goes away
and we're no longer
judged by skin color.

My Brotha

Why are you against me, my Brotha?
you would think that it is I
who has caused your pain and suffering
when in fact I too am a victim of society's rage
I just choose not to give in to it

Am I wrong for wanting more, my Brotha?
I only want my share of the common dream
instead of trying to keep us both down
you should be going for your share as well
because it's not going to come to you

Isn't there enough evil in the world, my Brotha?
as if things weren't bad enough
you're trying to sell your soul for drugs
all you get is more of the same pain and suffering
to feed your empty bitterness

Why are you feeling sorry for yourself, my Brotha?
you must look in the mirror to place blame
once you see what is really there you can begin again
to find the life you're dying to live
instead of living to die

If I can't trust you, my Brotha, then who?
we should be looking out for each other
and instead I feel related to the enemy
a stab in the back hurts more than a stab in the heart
because you don't see it coming
Turn around before it's too late,
my Brotha.

My Sista

Why do you compete with me, my Sista?
it shouldn't matter to you how light or dark I am
or how straight or curly my hair is
we are still from the same beautiful mold
that makes us separate but equal

Am I such a threat to you, my Sista?
you refuse to share your home with me
yet you share secrets that should never be told
you are quick to judge and misjudge others
but you refuse to look at yourself

Aren't there enough problems to deal with, my Sista?
our war should not be with each other
but with those who try to break our free spirit
let's not help them by trying to control
lives that are not our own

Why do you try so hard to belong, my Sista?
that will only encourage the rejection you fear
stop criticizing my progress and make your own
by learning to love yourself from within
you won't have to do without

If I can't turn to you, my Sista, then who?
we should be supporting each other
and instead I feel closer to the enemy
a stab in the heart hurts more than a stab in the back
because you can see who it's coming from
Wake up and face the truth,
my Sista.

Who Am I?

I AM Malcolm X with a vision
Martin Luther with a dream
Joe Louis with a glove
Michael Jordon and Kareem

Born into slavery
Reborn into freedom
to take my rightful place
in God's diversity kingdom
Who am I?

I AM Sharon Pratt Dixon
Frederick Douglass, Margaret Wilson
Shirley Chisholm, Langston Hughes
Ross in *Lady Sings the Blues*

Medgar Evers, Jesse Jackson
Louie Armstrong, Toni Braxton
Willie Brown, Colin Powell
Judith Jameson, Diahann Carroll
Who am I?

I AM Thurgood Marshall with a gavel
Nelson Mandela with a cause
Lena Horne with good jazz
Ella Fitzgerald and Lou Rawls

Thirsting for the knowledge
hungry for respect
searching for the answers
to support my intellect
Who am I?

I AM Miles Davis and Bob Marley
Bishop Kelly, Marcus Garvey
Dorothy Dandridge, Leontyne Price
Bo Jackson and Jerry Rice

Morris Chestnut, Stevie Wonder
Etta James, the Nicholas Brothers
Cecil Williams, Dorothy I. Height
always fighting for our rights
Who am I?

I AM Aretha Franklin with respect
Vanessa Williams without shame
Whitney Houston with good love
Carl Weathers, Satchel Paige

Shunned by racial boundaries
yet gained the right to vote
found praise and recognition
and the right to hope
Who am I?

I AM Susan L. Taylor, Alex Haley
Terri McMillan, Alvin Ailey
Thomas Bradley, Matthew Henson
Harriet Tubman and George Benson

Morgan Freeman, Gregory Hines
Mario Van Peebles, Wesley Snipes
Denzel Washington, Bernie Casey
Sammy Davis Jr. and Halle Berry
Who am I?

I AM Alice Walker with a story
Maya Angelou with a poem
Hank Aaron with a home run
Damon Wayans, Jesse Owens

Overwhelmed by outside envy
second-guessed by all
forever pushed and prodded
yet forever standing tall
Who am I?

I AM Oprah Winfrey, Allen Payne
Whoopi Goldberg, Marvin Gaye
William Cosby, Janet Jackson
Willie Kennedy, Debbie Allen

Who am I?
I AM a blessed child of God
on His solid rock I stand
strong, willing, and able
a proud, Black, African American.

See Me

the next time you see me
try not to notice
that my hair is naturally wavy
and doesn't need relaxing, pressing, or perming
—a gift from my father
or that my vanilla-colored skin
is kissed with a hint of caramel
maintained without benefit of a tanning booth
—a gift from my mother

the next time you see me
try not to notice
my confusion as I try to complete forms
that refer to me only as "other"
or the blinding ignorance
of those who hate me
even though they don't know me
they just know I'm not like them

the next time you see me
try not to notice
the looks of betrayal from black men
when they see me with a white man
or the hostile glances of white men
when they see me with a black man
and the enraged looks of women
who see me only as a threat

the next time you see me
try not to notice
the puffiness of my cried-out eyes
my frustration as I struggle to fit in, to belong
or the envy that consumes me
because you're more accepted than I am
and the desolate feeling of being an outcast
even when I'm standing in a crowd

the next time you see me
just see **Me**.

Beneath My Skin

If you look beneath my skin
you'll see the real person within
and that bigotry and hate
have not determined my true fate
If you look beneath my skin
an understanding will begin
and a cultural respect
will support your intellect
If you look beneath my skin
there's a past I won't defend
it won't be hard to just envision
a world without racial collision
If you look beneath my skin
you'll find the views that I intend
to share with those who'll benefit
from my African descent
If you look beneath my skin
you'll see a certain discipline
that allows me to adjust
when confronted with mistrust
If you look beneath my skin
it won't be hard to comprehend
why I fight until exhaust
against social holocaust

If you look beneath my skin
you'll find that time and time again
people tend to look at only
what closed minds have taught them solely
  If you look beneath my skin
you'll see concern that's genuine
about the world's state of affairs
and social pollutants in the air
  If you look beneath my skin
there is a power wearing thin
we need more than just one voice
fighting for freedom of choice
  If you look beneath my skin
you won't be looking out, but in
your vision will come clearer
as you venture to draw nearer
  If you look beneath my skin
years of suffering will mend
the world would be a better place
without disruption over race.

I Will Not Give In

It's really not a mystery
    what happened to Black History
    When you look inside "their" books
    it's no surprise we're overlooked
    Still with my patience wearing thin
    I know that I must not give in
It's a shame that in this nation
    some still cause humiliation
    All this worry over race
    has left in me a bitter taste
    But the pride I have within
    will not allow me to give in
When Martin Luther led the march
    his words of truth rang from all parts
    His dream was to let freedom ring
    and though he's gone now we still sing
    "Free At Last" all of God's children
    free at last to not give in
When my people were enslaved
    their heads held high until their graves
    Victims of hatred and disgust

by those who knew true prejudice
They held their pain by discipline
and I too will not give in
When Rosa Parks would not stand up
all of the world fell in disrupt
She held her ground until we won
but our real work is yet undone
A true-blood heroine
and like her I will not give in
I will not give in
years of segregation
vile abuse and degradation
I will not give in
verbal slurs so racial
hateful stares so glacial
I will not give in
words behind my back
dignity attacks
I will not give in
to the darkness of their sin.

African Queen (for Ndeye)

Behold her beauty
      the African Queen
      her ebony essence
      and nubian theme
      proud and intelligent
      decisive and more
      regal and royal
      for all to adore
Milk chocolate skin
      so creamy and smooth
      alluring, seductive
      with nothing to prove
      her lips so full
      and able to please
      hips that bring grown men
      down to their knees
So bold and so daring
      eyes sparkling like fire
      come savor the flavor
      of her hot desire
      soft to the touch
      from her toes to her hair
      journey inside her
      and she'll take you there
She's strong and she's sexy
      deliciously sweet
      come feel her fever
      come taste her meat
      the sister of sisters
      and second to none
      the African Queen
      she is truly the One.

Chapter 4

Journey to
Faith

"Always let your faith be stronger than your fear."—Gail Tennyson Hicks

God Answers Prayers

I know God answers prayers
for His miracles abound
my life is in His care
and I know it's safe and sound
When I add up all the blessings
He has bestowed upon my life
I am never left with guessing
how I conquered all my strife
The glory when He calls
will be for all the world to know
He loves us one and all
for the bible tells us so
He made you and He made me
He made the flowers bloom in May
He made the oceans and the seas
and He made each and every day
When you call Him, He will answer
and your faith will be restored
He will be your loving master
and love you to your very core

If your spirit is tattered and broken
your strength will be renewed
when your silent prayer is spoken
He will help you make it through
        He will comfort you and keep you
in times of trouble and despair
when you've done all that you can do
He will take it right from there
        And when you're at your best
it is to Him you should be thankful
praise Him more—not less
and vow forever to be grateful
        Follow His many teachings
for the lessons are worth learning
if you find that you're still seeking
it is for Him that you are yearning
        So, if you ever feel alone
don't worry—He is always there
celebrate the faith you've grown
remember that God answers prayers.

Black Hope

It puts food on our tables
clothes on our backs
and when things get tough
it picks up the slack

It's what springs eternal
with a soulful twist
and what puts success
at the head of our list

It's the difference between
half empty and half full
and puts faith in the hearts
of those without pull

It's what we do for the best
with an ebony flair
to comfort each other
and strengthen our prayers

It's the reason we struggle
and come out on top
the reason we work hard
and why success we adopt

It's the light at the end
of a tunnel of cope
our silver lining of clouds
we call it Black Hope.

Do Not Despair

Do not despair, my lonely dear friend
things just begin when they seem to end
you may think that today offers you little hope
but you have grown stronger while learning to cope

Do not wallow in pity, or give up on life
hold no place in your heart for stress or for strife
believe things will get better and pray that they do
and soon what you prayed for will come to be true

Do not envy others, but their courage admire
channel your energy to aim and reach higher
turn pain into power, turn loss into gain
turn hate into love, and your strength will remain

Do not let life infect you with negative thoughts
trust in your instinct to teach and be taught
control situations that get out of hand
defeat adversaries when in your way they stand

Do not dwell on the past, but look straight ahead
concentrate on the here, now, and later instead
be good to yourself, and things will soon change
a wisdom will surface with time and with age

So do not despair, my lonely dear friend
things will begin when they seem to end
although its not promised, tomorrow is there
and along with it comes someone special to care.

Sista!

Open up, look inside!
see the real you with pride!
you're so special and unique
you have that "something" others seek

Is it your charm? Is it your grace?
Is it the beauty of your face?
You're a Sista and you know it
and with every move you show it

Confidence not cowardice
add "a leader" to the list
honest, smart, sincere, and cool
a true friend and no one's fool

You've got it all with some to spare
and always take the time to share
Is it your voice? Is it your lips?
Is it the movement of your hips?

You're a Sista and "you go girl"
run on out and rule this world
giving all a chance to know
sweet success from head to toe

Your walk demands attention
and lest I forget to mention
that your eyes reveal your soul
and we know you're in control

Is it your laugh? Is it your smile?
Is it self-love that makes you wild?
You're a Sista and you're "all that"
a true diva, strong and steadfast

Your classy way speaks for itself
and you possess an inner wealth
a wealth of peace, a wealth of love
a wealth of faith in God above

It's YOU I want to celebrate
my Sista, 'cause I think you're great
we've got a bond that's beyond measure
Sistahood is a rare treasure.

God's House

Burn, baby burn

we knew what transpired

the smoke told us all

God's house was on fire

Tormented by flames

devastated and drowned

it was scorched inside out

and charred to the ground

It burned and it burned

until nothing remained

we watched 'til the end

our faces unchanged

When the walls crumbled

we held our heads high

when the ceilings tumbled

our tears stayed inside

Evil took over

where there was once good

it destroyed the foundation

where God's house once stood

Why do they hate us?

why burn down our place?

the place where we worship

the place where we wait

They can't burn the truth

that they choose to ignore

they can't burn the plan

that God has in store

They can't burn our faith

not now and not ever

they can't burn the hope

that holds us together

Although we rebuild

we shall not be soothed

although they keep pushing

we shall not be moved

In the end what is just

shall rise and prevail

God will be with us

and they'll go to hell.

Anyway

Skin sprinkled with moles
chipped teeth
scarred neck
too much tummy
not enough butt
overabundant hips
cellulite thighs
crooked feet
jacked up toes
thank you
for loving me
anyway.

I Am Woman

I am woman, hear me roar
knocking down oppression's door

Smart, successful, strong and able
let me tell you of my fable . . .

Once submersed in poverty
My only friend was misery

I could not read, I could not write
my circumstances held me tight

I lived in shelters here and there
helped by those who thought to care

One day as I was passing by
my own reflection caught my eye

I did not like the sight I saw
but it put writing on the wall

I went to sleep and woke up smart
set out to make a brand new start

Learned to read and went to school
no longer will I be a fool

Got a job and saved my money
now I'm more than milk and honey

I worked hard and on my own
bought myself a brand new home

I've grasped the silent victory
and earned my place in history

I've paid my debt and paid my dues
No longer will I be abused

Now what you see is what you get
they haven't broken my spirit yet

I've got my self-respect, you see
and faith has set my spirit free.

It's Just God

Whenever I'm in turmoil
    faced with adversity
    I know with all my heart
    it's just God testing me
Whenever I get called on
    to help a friend in need
    I try my best to be there
    it's just God using me
Whenever I can learn from
    the lessons I receive
    I always feel so grateful
    it's just God teaching me
Whenever I need comfort
    from all my many worries
    an inner strength emerges
    it's just God embracing me
Whenever I am thankful
    rapt in spiritual harmony
    my prayers are always answered
    it's just God blessing me
Whenever I remain
    true to myself, I'm free
    I know that I am His
    it's just God loving me.

Strength

Lord, give me strength
    it's what I need to get by
    as I struggle to get through
    on you I rely
Lord, give me strength
    each day I awake
    with the kindness to give
    and the courage to take
Lord, give me strength
    to see things a new way
    and gently remind me
    of tomorrow's new day
Lord, give me strength
    to not feel so alone
    teach me to go your way
    instead of my own
Lord, give me strength
    to accept the past
    and to know from experience
    the bad times don't last
Lord, give me strength
    in all that I do
    in Your Son's name I pray
    and with love, I thank You.

Beauty

Ever wonder
how God makes
the world so beautiful
the flowers, trees
birds and bees
so glorious and humble
they say beauty is in
the beholder's eye
but I think its everywhere
you just have to try
to see it all around you
and embrace its cause
it's meant to give us reverence
it's meant to give us pause
the mountains, the snow
the fields and the streams
all places to adore

all places to dream
the lakes, the valleys
nature at its best
enjoying it all
is our life test
take a moment and stop
then get to know
the rays of summer's heat
or walk in winter's snow
smell the daisies
in the spring
crush the leaves
in the fall
or just sit back
and marvel
at the beauty
of it all.

The Key to Success

If you think you can win
when all else is lost
If you think you can pay
in spite of the cost
If you know in your heart
that you've done your best
That's when you'll **EXPLORE**
the key to success.

If you stumble and fall
then stand up again
If you strive hard to grasp
what you don't understand
If you trust in your instincts
to pass your life test
That's when you'll **DISCOVER**
the key to success.

If you gamble the risk
and come out on top
If you're willing to start
when all others stop
If you face your worst fear
without second-guess
That's when you'll **LEARN**
the key to success.

If you master integrity
and a sense of fair play
If you open your mind
to more than one way
If you honor what's true
and reject hopelessness
That's when you'll **KNOW**
the key to success.

If you're tired of following
and instead take the lead
If you set out to earn
all in life that you need
If you strive to give more
but not settle for less
That's when you'll **HAVE**
the key to success.

If you look for the right
in a world full of wrong
If you discover the faith
that you've had all along
If you look to the Lord
to take care of the rest
That's when you'll **MASTER**
the key to success.

Chapter 5

Journey to
Me

"I pray that I never look like what I've been through."
—Gail Tennyson Hicks

I Am

I am who I am
should I apologize?
hold my head in shame
or wear a fake disguise
Am I to ignore
my brown colored skin
to make others feel good
about the skin that they're in
Am I not to acknowledge
my ample round hips
or my not-so-straight hair
and my full, juicy lips
Should I turn away
from the slaves in my past
from their hurt and shame
and their agonized masks
Should I dishonor my brothas
and betray my sistas
to look like the others
the misses and mistas

Should I take the Lord's name
in slander and vain
to try to fit into
a world that's insane?
No!
I am who I am!
I will not apologize
I will hold my head up
and look them in the eyes
I will not ignore
my hair, color, or hips
I will not feel bad
about my full, juicy lips
But I will stand tall
like my ancestors did
to honor a history
that we still live in
the Lord I will take
as my savior instead
of living a life
that is better off dead.

Real

What's real?
what's real is that
this is Me
if you don't like what you see
keep steppin'
'cause I am not here to
please you
appease you
or beseech you
you are not going to
reform Me
conform Me
or try to "norm" Me
what's real is that you cannot
change Me
estrange Me
or alienate Me
'cause I'm a sista
with a pencil and I'll blow you away

with my words 'cause I don't play
the things you say
behind my back
your precious personal attack
does nothing more than
bruise my ego
but it doesn't touch my soul
or take its toll
and you ain't nuthin' but a half-people
'cause only half-people
have to talk badly
about someone else
in order to feel whole
and I can't resist
feeling sorry that you exist
because I'd rather feel
nothing at all
but what's real
is that I do.

Make Room

Why don't you see me as I really am
not whom you think I used to be?
those misconceptions came
from many, many distorted years ago
founded in fiction
fried into fact
served as a knife
in the middle of my back
and were you so perfect then?
I think not . . . I know not
your assumptions annoy me
like rusty nails
screeching
across the chalkboard of my mind
your accusations destroy me
until I realize that I never did the things
you thought I did
the truth conveniently hidden

faith in me forbidden
why is it so easy
to find fault in me
without first finding it in you?
because only when you see your true self
can you dare to look at someone else
and even then
you won't see all that is there
like an incomplete stare
so don't presume
make room
for the certainty that you are fallible
make room
for the possibility that you are gullible
make room
for what you don't see
make room
for me.

My New Friend

Reality came by today
she knocked
and when I opened the door
she floated in
like a cool breeze
on a warm day
she gently turned me
so that I faced her
and showed me things
things I had long forgotten
let go of
or conveniently denied
startled, I tried to run
but Reality held me softly
and told me it would be alright
she eased my rose-colored glasses off
so that I could see more clearly
that what I thought all along

really wasn't meant to be
she showed me
that what really was
wasn't so bad
and that I was blessed
nevertheless
we talked of the past
of the loves that didn't last
we talked of the present
and the things that made me hesitant
we talked of the future
about dreamers and doers
my tears flowed freely
because I was now free
I thanked my new friend
she smiled, dried my eyes and left
with the promise to return
whenever I needed to see her again.

Selfish

How dare you call me selfish
when all I did was try
to be the best that I could be
and the twinkle in your eye

How dare you call me selfish
when you I worshipped near and far
but you've changed so drastically that
I don't know now who you are

How dare you call me selfish
when my family is my strength
you would know that if you knew me
but the time you never spent

How dare you call me selfish
when you alienated all of us
your outbursts and your tantrums
leaving trails of bitter disgust

How dare you call me selfish
when you're the one concerned
with what others can do for you
and whose reputation you can burn

How dare you call me selfish
when all you have to do
is look in any mirror and see
the selfish one is you.

Don't Be Afraid of the Fat Girl

I wasn't always fat
I used to be "pleasingly plump"
before that I was "thick and juicy"
before that I was "healthy"
and before that I was a perfect Size 12

Now that Size 12 is long way off

Learning to love myself
in spite of what the scale read
was a long, drawn-out
knock-down, hair-pulling
kneecap-kicking battle
between my self esteem and my ego

Meanwhile
I cried, I prayed
I read my Essence magazine
I read my Acts of Faith
and I attended every encouraging
uplifting, self-acceptance
workshop I could find

Now I love me anyway
just the way I am
and the last time I checked
so did my family, my friends
and my husband and sons

I may not ever make it back to Size 12
but I made it back to me
and that's what matters most

Now, 'scuse me while
I have some cake . . .

Judgment Day

Remember the times
when you judged me so wrongly
accusing me of evil sins
as if I were the only

While you sat there so perfect
your faults carefully hidden
in your chair of royal values
all of your sins God-forgiven

Not realizing that true friendship
allows for imperfections
it requires pure acceptance
not betrayal and rejection

You forgot it's not your job
to judge what other people do
you forgot to be the true friend
I had always been to you

Instead you chose to lose
the best friend you ever had
and then you had the nerve
to feel justified and glad

If you knew what this really cost you
your pride would take off running
but it's too late now and by the way—
your judgment day is coming.

I Will Survive (Tribute to Maya)

You may stab me in the back
for reasons that you try to hide
you may publicly accuse me
but like the earth, I will survive

Are you shocked by my conviction
overwhelmed by my good sense
'cause I have no time to let you
undermine my confidence

Like the mountains and the trees
that keep growing tall and wide
like a wounded vet from war
again and again, I will survive

Would you rather see me fail
just give up and hope to die
do you want me to stop reaching
for that ribbon in the sky

Does my attitude alarm you
you may think that I am strange
'cause I don't have time to sit around
and watch you play your games

You may threaten to do harm to me
or try to hurt my pride
you may verbally assault me
but like the ocean, I will survive

Do you sometimes sit and wonder
how to get me to break down
'cause I act like nothing hurts me
as I boldly stare you down

Through the troubles of the world
I will survive
all the insults life may hurl
I will survive
I am full of beauty and grace
God has put me in this place

Through long lost loves and broken hearts
I will survive
from new beginnings turned to false starts
I will survive
I am a Black woman, strong and proud
dispelling the myths, removing the doubt
I will survive . . .
I will survive . . .
I will survive.

Love Yourself

Be not dismayed
by your reflection in the mirror
for it only shows what you look like
not who you really are
sometimes we fool ourselves
into thinking that if we look good on the outside
that will make us a better person
on the inside

But it doesn't work like that
because if you put a rotten apple in a box
and wrap it in the prettiest paper you could find
that won't change the fact that there is still
a rotten apple inside the box
Will it? No, it won't.

The key is to be the best person
that you can be on the inside
and to love yourself, because doing so
will make you look better than anything
you could ever do
to aid your outward appearance.

When you love yourself, there is a presence about you
a powerful glow from within that says you are at peace
with all your faults limitations, and imperfections
because you know that in spite of these things
you are still wonderful
Aren't you? Yes, you are.

And if you believe this
others will too
because they will see it
in the way you walk, talk
and do the things you do
Won't they?
Yes, they will.

I Am Fine!

From my head
down to my toes
I've got a fineness
going on
it may be
the way I walk
or the intelligent
way I talk
one thing is for sure
I've got it going on
for good
I couldn't stop it
if I tried
I cannot help it
if I'm fine
on days when
it is raining
on days when
there is shine
even on my Ugly Days
you'll see that
I'm still fine
my luscious lips
and caramel skin
confidence glowing
from within
sweet like cherries
potent like wine
just can't help it

I'm so damn fine
neither ten pounds lost
nor ten pounds gained
can take away from
my gorgeous frame
my age don't matter
because I know
whatever the number
my fineness will show
if you know me
then you love me
if you don't
you surely won't
for it's too late
to catch up to me
best settle for
reflections of me
have no doubt
of my success
don't put your ego
to the test
I have arrived
and here to stay
don't let your pride
get in my way
I am a queen
who will not hide
the fact that is
that I am fine!

Journey

I've made mistakes, yes
but I have no regrets
the lessons I've learned
I try not to forget

But I've also had triumphs
too many to name
I'm proud of this journey
that God sent my way

Life's changes and challenges
the ebb and the flow
all serve the purpose
of helping me grow

True friends I have many
what blessings they are
they light up my life
each one a bright star

I also have family
adding joy to my days
those who stood by me
faith rooted and stayed

I remain ever grateful
as God leads me through
and look forward to each day
as my journey continues.